UNDERSTANDING
TOBACCO

UPFRONT HEALTH

D1497402

Published in the United States of America by Cherry Lake Publishing
Ann Arbor, Michigan
www.cherrylakepublishing.com

Reading Adviser: Marla Conn MS, Ed., Literacy specialist, Read-Ability, Inc.

Photo Credits: ©ToprakBeyBetmen/Getty Images, cover; ©Rubberball/Mike Kemp/Getty Images, 1; ©Nenov/Getty Images, 5; ©Sebastian Kaulitzki/Shutterstock, 9; ©DougSchneiderPhoto/Getty Images, 10; ©iStockphoto/Getty Images, 12; ©HEX/Getty Images, 15; ©Tim Boyle/Getty Images, 19; ©Image Point Fr/Shutterstock, 20; ©Hollie Fernando/Getty Images, 23; ©IVL/Shutterstock, 25; ©Steve Smith/Getty Images, 27; ©kumikomini/Getty Images, 28; ©Nenov/Getty Images, 30

Library of Congress Cataloging-in-Publication Data has been filed and is available at catalog.loc.gov

Cherry Lake Publishing would like to acknowledge the work of The Partnership for 21st Century Learning.
Please visit *www.p21.org* for more information.

Printed in the United States of America
Corporate Graphics

ABOUT THE AUTHOR

Matt Chandler is the author of more than 35 non-fiction children's books. He lives in New York with his wife Amber and his children Zoey and Oliver. When he isn't busy researching or writing his next book, Matt travels the country bringing his school author visits and writing workshops to elementary and middle school students.

TABLE OF CONTENTS

The World of Tobacco

Smoking in the United States and Canada has declined in recent years, but it has been replaced with an equally deadly alternative, electronic cigarettes. Using electronic cigarettes, also known as vaping, eliminates the smoke and the bad taste of cigarettes. Unfortunately, it doesn't eliminate the addictive **nicotine**. According to the Centers for Disease Control, more than 20 percent of high school students surveyed in 2018 admitted to using electronic cigarettes.

Whether you smoke a traditional cigarette, puff on an e-cigarette, or use chewing tobacco, the nicotine and chemicals can be deadly. When you take that first puff, a lot happens to your body. The **dopamine** release is just one part of the

Nicotine is found in the tobacco plant, mostly the leaves.

physical reaction. Within 20 minutes, the nicotine enters your bloodstream. This highly addictive, toxic chemical is carried throughout your body, spreading the damage that can be done. Most people know that smoking is bad for your lungs. But the nicotine and chemicals found in cigarettes and vape juice impact more than your breathing. Once the chemicals enter your bloodstream they are carried to every organ, muscle, and tissue in your body. The damage can be fast, and in some cases, deadly.

Smoking Expenses

Smoking is a deadly habit. It is also an expensive one. In New York City, a pack of cigarettes costs $13. Many people who smoke consume one pack every day. That's more than $4,700 each year to smoke!

Studies show that 72 percent of smokers live in lower-income communities. Why would the people who can least afford to smoke have the highest rate of smoking? Because for years, tobacco companies have targeted low-income neighborhoods and young people. Do some research on the internet. Find three ways the tobacco industry has targeted people who can't afford to smoke. Do you think these methods should be legal?

People often think it takes a long time to become addicted to smoking or vaping. The truth is your body can develop a dependency on the nicotine found in tobacco products very quickly. While smoking or vaping, your brain enjoys the feeling that nicotine gives it. However, within a few minutes of finishing a cigarette, those effects can wear off. Without the chemicals inhaled from the cigarette, people begin to feel irritable and anxious. Or they might feel sleepy and "crash"

[21ST CENTURY SKILLS LIBRARY]

from the withdrawal. Those feelings of "crashing" will increase each time you smoke a cigarette or vape until you reach **addiction**.

Vaping can be even worse. Because it tastes so good and is easy to use, young people can vape more than they might smoke a cigarette. This can lead to taking in more nicotine in a day than if they smoked traditional cigarettes.

Are Anti-Smoking Campaigns Working?

Smoking rates in the United States and Canada continue to decline. In 2017, just 16.2 percent of Canadians surveyed smoked daily or occasionally. In the United States, that number was 14 percent. Both countries have invested millions of dollars in anti-smoking campaigns. There are many countries across the globe where smoking rates are much higher. More than 50 percent of adult men in China smoke. Can you find three other countries with higher rates of smoking than Canada and the United States? What do you think causes some countries to have more smokers?

The Effects of Smoking

A person who smokes one pack per day for 30 years will smoke 219,000 cigarettes in his or her lifetime. Each cigarette is packed with addictive nicotine, **tar**, and thousands of chemicals. That smoke goes straight to your lungs, where it is absorbed into the tissue. Over time, the person's airways can become blocked and breathing becomes difficult. After a lifetime of smoking, many people have to wear oxygen to breathe.

Smoking affects your entire body, not just your lungs. When you smoke, it changes your brain. Your brain develops extra nicotine **receptors**, and if you try to quit, your brain reacts to the withdrawal. Headaches, nausea, anxiety, and depression can all be side effects.

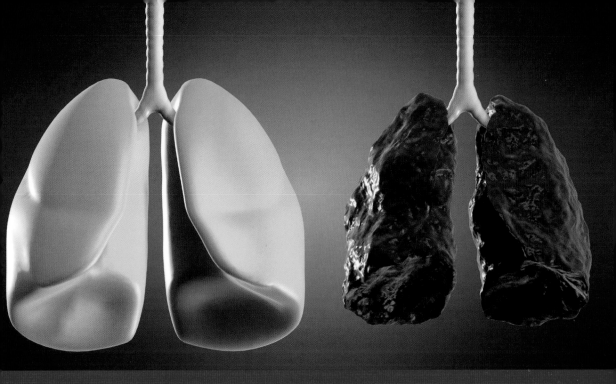

Almost 90 percent of deaths from lung cancer are due to smoking.

Longtime smokers may have trouble seeing, especially at night. Those who smoke also have an increased chance of developing **cataracts**. Hearing loss can also be a side effect. That's because long-term smoking reduces oxygen to the inner-ear. These are all troubling and sometimes scary outcomes from smoking, but the biggest risk for those who smoke is cancer.

There are many types of cancer directly connected to smoking. Many of them are **fatal**. The most common cancers with a connection to smoking are cancer of the lungs, throat, stomach, pancreas, bladder, kidneys, colon, and cervix.

Most states in the United States have comprehensive laws that ban smoking from certain indoor and outdoor areas.

New smokers also suffer from short-term side effects of this deadly habit. First, there are the social side effects. Laws have made it illegal to smoke in offices, at sporting events, in restaurants, and in many other public places. People are forced to leave their friends to go outside and have a cigarette. Many families don't allow smoking in the house. Imagine being at Thanksgiving dinner and a relative has to keep leaving to go outside and smoke. Smoking can be a very isolating habit. It also gives you bad breath, and your clothes and hair will smell.

Then there are the physical effects. Smokers will begin to feel a shortness of breath during physical activities. Running, playing sports, or even walking up flights of stairs can leave you feeling out of breath. Smokers may also experience an elevated heart rate as their bodies work harder to pump blood. Short-term smoking can also lead to an increased risk of asthma.

Getting You Hooked

Cigarettes make you sick, and they can kill you. So how do tobacco companies get millions of people to smoke? Tobacco companies use powerful advertising techniques. In 2016, tobacco companies spent $9.5 billion in marketing and advertising. They gave away free clothes, electronics, and other swag with their cigarettes. They heavily advertised their products in lower-income neighborhoods. Also, tobacco companies know that people with less money often quit smoking if the cost gets too high. They use a majority of their marketing dollars to give cash **rebates** *to the people that sell their cigarettes. This allows stores in low-income neighborhoods to lower prices and keep people hooked on tobacco.*

There are more than 7,000 chemicals in second-hand smoke. About 70 of the chemicals are known to cause cancer.

Second-Hand Smoke

Tobacco can kill you even if you never smoke. Second-hand smoke contains dangerous chemicals. It is estimated that since 1964, more than 2.5 million non-smokers have died from complications from exposure to second-hand smoke.

A total of 43 states have laws banning smoking in workplaces. Some local lawmakers have even banned smoking in cars if there is a child present. Do you think adults have a right to smoke? Should the government be allowed to ban people from smoking in their own cars? Do some research to support your opinion.

12

About 443,000 U.S. Deaths Attributable Each Year to Cigarette Smoking*

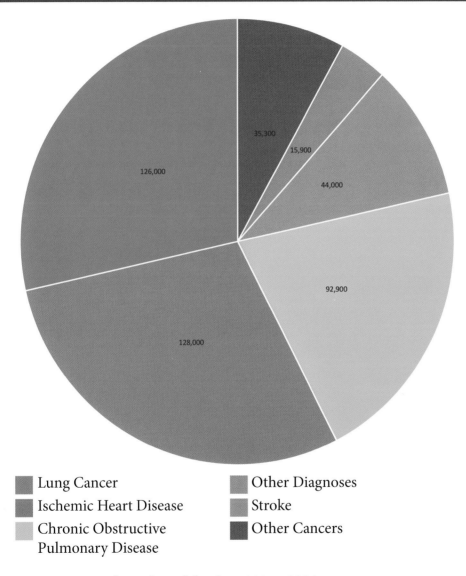

Lung Cancer
Ischemic Heart Disease
Chronic Obstructive Pulmonary Disease
Other Diagnoses
Stroke
Other Cancers

*Average annual number of deaths, 2000 to 2004.

Source: MMWR 2008;57(45):1226-1228.

E-Cigarettes and Teens

E-cigarettes, vaping, vape pens, e-hookahs, or e-juice. In every form, they are fast becoming an **epidemic** among young people. Electronic cigarettes are battery operated. They are filled with a liquid that is usually flavored. The device heats the liquid into a mist and the user inhales it like a cigarette, then exhales. Because there is no smoke or foul smell, some people falsely believe electronic cigarettes are not bad for you. While it is true these products don't have tar, nor as many chemicals as are found in cigarettes, they are still not good for you.

E-cigarettes have only been available since 2003. Scientists and medical experts don't have clear data on the long-term effects of vaping. One thing that is certain: It may taste good,

E-cigarettes can contain just as much nicotine as traditional cigarettes. Some e-cigarettes have 10 times more nicotine.

but vaping still delivers a dose of nicotine to the user's bloodstream. Nicotine is what makes traditional cigarettes addictive and deadly. E-cigarette users can control how much nicotine they receive. Extra-strength cartridges release higher levels of nicotine. Users can also raise the voltage in the electronic cigarette. This gives off a stronger dose each time they inhale.

Vaping can also cause problems with brain development in teens. The human brain isn't fully developed until around age 25. Before then, introducing nicotine and chemicals found in

Popcorn Lung

One of the most serious side effects of vaping is a condition known as "popcorn lung." Don't let the name fool you—popcorn lung is a painful condition linked to diacetyl, a chemical used to add flavor to vaping juice. A 2015 study tested 51 flavored e-cigarettes and found diacetyl in 39 of them! Diacetyl was originally used to flavor microwave popcorn, which is how this painful condition got its name.

Bronchioles are tiny passages in your lungs where oxygen passes through. In people with popcorn lung, those passages get irritated and swollen. This blocks the air from getting through. People with popcorn lung struggle to breathe and can suffer permanent damage to their lungs.

e-cigarettes into the brain could cause delays in brain development. E-cigarettes can contain heavy metals including lead, as well as chemicals that have been linked to cancer.

So why did more than 1 in 5 high school students surveyed say they have vaped? Vaping is easier. Cigarettes leave evidence in the form of smoke. It's easier to sneak a puff on a vape. Then there are the different flavors that attract teens. Inhaling flavorings such as cotton candy, cinnamon roll, or butterscotch taste good. The biggest factor may be a lack of education. Multiple studies have found that teens think vaping is safe. Many even think they are doing a good thing by vaping instead of smoking cigarettes. Unfortunately, a study from Yale University found teen users of e-cigarettes are more likely to smoke regular cigarettes later in life.

From Smoking to Vaping

There was a time when smoking cigarettes was seen as "cool." Kids smoked to rebel against their parents. But thanks to aggressive anti-smoking campaigns and positive education programs in school, smoking has lost its cool factor.

*Today, "vaping" has replaced cigarettes among teens. With nearly 8,000 flavors, vaping is designed to appeal to kids. E-cigarettes are also designed to be fashionable, and in some cases, to trick unsuspecting adults. **JUUL** devices look, at first glance, like a flash drive. Students can keep them in their backpacks or even in their desks at school with less fear of being caught. There have even been reports of students puffing discreetly on their JUUL in school. Studies show that a JUUL device delivers more nicotine per puff than a cigarette.*

CHAPTER 4

Ending the Epidemic

What can be done to stop young people from smoking and help current smokers quit? There is no magic answer. Nicotine is as addictive as heroin, so quitting is difficult. Reaching young people before they pick up a cigarette or a vape for the first time is crucial. There are two primary ways to address the epidemic.

Education: Public education has already made big strides in cutting smoking rates. Between 2005 and 2016, the number of smokers in the United States dropped 25 percent. The U.S. **Surgeon General** credits anti-smoking public service campaigns with the drop in smoking. Today, the focus of that education needs to shift. Young people who would never consider smoking a cigarette are addicted to their vape pen. The anti-smoking model that has been so effective to educate people

The top tobacco companies spend almost $9 billion each year on marketing.

about the dangers of smoking needs to be applied to e-cigarettes.

Government Regulations: In 2012, one study found that 80 percent of teen smokers smoked one of the three most-advertised cigarette brands. Teens are influenced by advertising. The government has placed heavy restrictions on tobacco advertising. In the 1970s, cigarette advertisements were banned from television and radio. In 1998, the government banned advertising them on billboards and at sporting events. Tobacco companies now devote most of their advertising money to

Nicotine patches and gum have about a 20 percent success rate. That means 80 percent of people start smoking again within one year.

convenience stores, gas stations, and retail stores that sell their products. Should the government ban all advertising of tobacco products?

Prevention is important, but what about the people who are ready to quit smoking or vaping? There are options to help. Some adults use nicotine replacement therapy, commonly known as "the patch." A smoker wears a patch on his or her body that releases small amounts of nicotine. This helps the person break the habit of smoking cigarettes and is said to ease withdrawal symptoms.

Federal law also requires most health insurance companies to cover medications, therapy, and other treatments designed to help people quit smoking. Many states also have programs to assist low-income individuals quit smoking. These programs can help pay for medication and therapy that may not be covered by insurance.

Breaking the Habit

Non-smokers might think quitting smoking is easy. But an addiction to anything can be painful to try and quit.

Do you have something you do every day? Drink soda? Text with your friends? Play video games? Pick something you do every day and try to go for one day without doing it. Pay attention to how you feel. Are you anxious? Do you miss it? Are you feeling any physical withdrawal? Write down any symptoms. Then go a second full day. It will get harder. Could you make it for an entire week?

A Social Element

For many people, smoking is a social habit. Social smokers may not smoke every day. Many young people smoke when they are offered a cigarette or a puff on their friend's vape. Others might take a puff or two from an e-cigarette at the end of the day to relax but never smoke any other time. Even though they might not consider themselves smokers, even casual smoking and vaping can cause serious health issues.

Each time you vape or smoke, it leaves behind chemicals, poisons, and nicotine in your system. Doctors and experts say each puff is doing serious damage, even for the casual smoker.

About 62 percent of people who smoke say
they are light or social smokers.

Making Good Choices

Do you have friends that smoke or vape? You may even have siblings or relatives who do. Peer pressure is a huge factor in teens smoking and vaping. If you are with your friends and everyone is passing a JUUL around, it might feel like you have to use it. You don't, but it is important to be prepared to respond.

Peer pressure doesn't mean friends are forcing you to smoke. With vaping, it can be tempting when you see how much fun your friends seem to be having. They look so relaxed and everyone is talking about how good the new juice tastes. If everyone in your group seems like they are having fun, it's

Saying "no" to peer pressure might be difficult in the moment, but it can save teens from a lifetime struggle with nicotine addiction.

natural to want to join in. But your brain can become addicted to nicotine after as little as one or two uses. Once you start, your brain will crave more nicotine, and it will be very hard to quit.

Besides peer pressure, young people model behavior they see at home. You've already learned about the dangers of second-hand smoke. In households where adults smoke, children are six times more likely to smoke. In one study, 29

How to Find Help

Quitting smoking is hard. Whether it's cigarettes, chewing tobacco, or vaping, these products are addictive. The good news is, there is help available. The first resource for you to learn about the dangers of smoking is your school health office. You can ask questions and get helpful information. The American Lung Association website is another good place to start. Cigarettes are the only product that, if used for their intended purpose, kill half of all long-term users. Vaping is highly addictive and damaging to your lungs. If you've started, you can stop. Make good choices every day to be tobacco-free.

percent of children whose parents smoked also took up smoking. In that same study, the rate of smoking among kids with non-smoking parents was just 8 percent. If you live in a home with people who smoke, pay attention to them. Do they cough a lot? Do they seem out of breath after doing basic activities? One way to avoid falling into the trap of smoking is to focus on the negative parts of the habit.

Teachers and school staff members can be a great resource
for information on tobacco and effective ways to say "no."

People who have supportive friends and family members are more successful when quitting tobacco.

In the United States and Canada, more than 700,000 people die annually from smoking-related illnesses. You don't want to be one of them. Smoking, vaping, or using chewing tobacco are all choices. Each choice comes with a deadly addiction and an increased chance of early death. You have a long life to live. Make it a tobacco-free life.

Could It Be Genetics?

Researchers from the Georgetown University Medical Center conducted two studies on how your **genetics** *may impact smoking. They found that subjects who had a specific dopamine transporting gene, SLC6A3-9, were less likely to smoke than those without the gene. The study also showed that smokers with the gene started smoking later in life and had more success quitting.*

Do your parents smoke? Did their parents smoke? Do some research and find out how many smokers you have in your family. How old were they when they started? Did any of them quit smoking?

Think About It

Tobacco used to only grow wild in North and South America and was farmed by Native Americans. People from Europe learned about it from Native Americans in the late 1400s. Before long, tobacco use spread across the world. Tobacco farming was a major part of the early United States. It continues to be a large part of American farming today.

Learn more about the history, development, and future of tobacco farming. Research the topic on the internet or at your local library. Do you think tobacco has been important to the United States? Or do you think the country would have been better off without it?

Learn More

BOOKS

Cornell, Kari A. *E-cigarettes and Their Dangers.* San Diego: ReferencePoint Press, 2019.

Esherick, Joan. *Smoking-Related Health Issues.* Broomall, PA: Mason Crest, 2014.

Gordon, Sherri Mabry. *Everything You Need to Know about Smoking, Vaping, and Your Health.* New York: Rosen Young Adult, 2019.

Mara, Wil. *Advertising.* Ann Arbor, MI: Cherry Lake Publishing, 2019.

ON THE WEB

GirlsHealth Ways to Say No
https://www.girlshealth.gov/substance/smoking/sayno.html

KidsHealth
https://kidshealth.org/en/teens/drug-alcohol/tobacco

Smoking Stinks Games
https://teens.smokingstinks.org/games

WHO Tobacco Free Initiative
https://www.who.int/tobacco/research/youth/health_effects/en

GLOSSARY

addiction (uh-DIK-shun) having no control over doing something, such as drugs or gambling, even though you know it is bad for your health and life

cataracts (KA-tuh-rakts) cloudy spots that form on a person's eye and makes it hard to see

dopamine (DOHP-uh-meen) a chemical in the brain that influences feelings of pleasure and emotions

epidemic (ep-i-DEM-ik) a health crisis that affects many people at once

fatal (FEI-tuhl) able to cause death

genetics (jen-ET-iks) the process of passing down qualities and characteristics, such as physical appearance and risk for disease, from parents to children

JUUL (JOOL) a brand of e-cigarette designed to look like a USB flash drive; JUUL batteries are recharged using a USB charger

nicotine (NIK-uh-teen) a poisonous chemical found in tobacco

rebate (REE-beyt) a partial refund given to someone after they purchased or paid too much for a product or service

receptor (ree-SEP-tohr) an organ or cell that perceives a change in the body and triggers a response

surgeon general (SUR-juhn JEN-ur-uhl) the head of public health services in the United States; the surgeon general is appointed by the president

tar (TAHR) a sticky brown substance created when tobacco is burned; tar is the primary cause of lung and throat cancer

INDEX